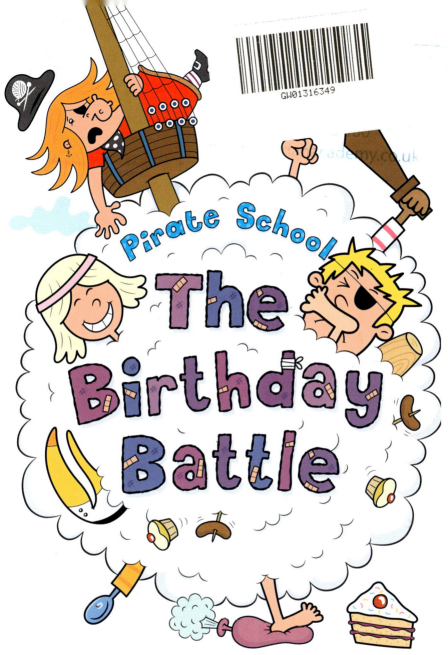

Pirate School

The Birthday Battle

Adapted from Pirate School: The Birthday Bash
by Jeremy Strong

Illustrated by Ian Cunliffe

Adapted by Maureen Haselhurst

Published by Pearson Education Limited, Edinburgh Gate, Harlow, Essex, CM20 2JE
Registered company number: 872828

www.pearsonschools.co.uk

Adapted text based on *Pirate School: The Birthday Bash*, originally published by Puffin Books Ltd in 2003.

Adaptation by Maureen Haselhurst

First published 2012

18
10 9 8

British Library Cataloguing in Publication Data
A catalogue record for this book is available from the British Library

ISBN 978 0 435 07604 7

Printed and bound in China by CTPS

Acknowledgements
We would like to thank the children and teachers of Bangor Central Integrated Primary School, NI; Barley Hill School, Thame; Bishop Henderson C of E Primary School, Somerset; Brookside Community Primary School, Somerset; Catcott Primary School, Somerset; Cheddington Combined School, Buckinghamshire; Cofton Primary School, Birmingham; Dair House Independent School, Buckinghamshire; Deal Parochial School, Kent; Lawthorn Primary School, North Ayrshire; Newbold Riverside Primary School, Rugby and Windmill Primary School, Oxford for their invaluable help in the development and trialling of the Bug Club resources.

Every effort has been made to contact copyright holders of material reproduced in this book. Any omissions will be rectified in subsequent printings if notice is given to the publisher.

Contents

Chapter 1
Pirate School

Pirate School is run by a nightmare on legs. Her name is Mrs Patagonia Clatterbottom.

Her nose is like an ancient potato.

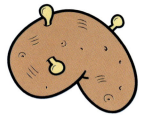

Her hands are like snapping lobsters.

She has a wooden leg and rides about in a boat-pram, shouting VERY LOUDLY!

All the children are afraid of her, except Ziggy, who's not scared of anything much. Even Miss Snitty, the school secretary, is afraid of bossy-boots Clatterbottom.

However, Pirate School lessons are exciting.

Mrs Muggwump teaches rope-swinging, Mad Maggott teaches walking the gangplank and Miss Fishgripp teaches capturing-skills – biffing and baffing and that kind of stuff.

They also have disco dancing lessons from a teacher called Jiggling Jim.

"Dancing is dead boring," said Smudge.

"It's dead stupid," sniggered Ziggy, who was wearing a pair of joke vampire fangs.

"Well, Corkella and I love dancing," said Flo, as Corkella went spinning overboard. SPLASH!

Mrs Clatterbottom hip-hopped past them on her wooden leg.

"I could have been a Disco Queen," she boasted

"No way," muttered Ziggy.

"I heard that, you horrible child!" she bellowed. "Aargh!"

6

Chapter 2
Dick Lurkin's School

Not very far from the Pirate School was Dick Lurkin's School for Highway-kids.

He taught them how to ride horses and say fierce, highway-kiddish things, like: "Stand and deliver, your money or your liver! Grrrrr!"

The highway-kids made masks to hide their faces. Then they would jump out of the woods and scare the pants off people. Oh, how they loved pinching pants.

Whenever they met the pirate kids there was sure to be a battle, but the highway-kids had always won. Until now …

Chapter 3
Presents for Patagonia

It was Patagonia Clatterbottom's birthday. "I feel like dancing," she bellowed. "Look at me! I'm a Disco Queen!" she yelled as she gave Jiggling Jim a twirl. In fact, it was such a mighty twirl that he went flying off and got stuck in the rigging.

"Leave him," ordered Mrs Clatterbottom. "What have you children got me for my birthday?"

Flo gave her a shell.

Smudge had made her a picture.

Corkella had saved her a sweet.

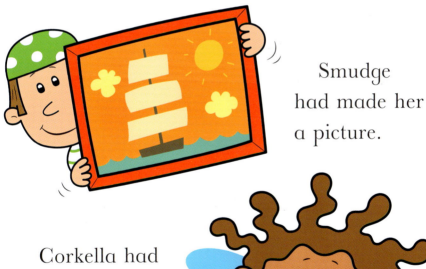

"Mine's a surprise," said Ziggy. "You'll have to sit down to get it."

Patagonia Clatterbottom greedily rubbed her hands and sat down where Ziggy pointed.

SPLRRRRRRGH!

"Throw that child overboard!" bellowed
Mrs Clatterbottom, but everyone was too
busy laughing.

"We're going to have a party," Mrs Clatterbottom announced. "We need plenty of pies and jelly. Smitty – to the shops!"

So off went the pirates, leaving poor Jiggling Jim stuck in the rigging. They bought heaps of pies and jelly from the shop.

"Yummy!" said Patagonia Clatterbottom. "This is going to be the best birthday bash ever!"

Chapter 4
The Ambush

On their way back from the shops, the pirates had to go through a wood and out jumped the highway-kids. WHAT A SHOCK!

"Stand and deliver. Your mummy or your liver. Grrr!" demanded Spotty Mask fiercely.

"But our mummies aren't here," Ziggy pointed out.

"Well, hand over your shopping then," snarled Daisy Mask.

"No way! That's my birthday feast," yelled Patagonia Clatterbottom.

"Tough bananas!" yelled Monkey Mask and the highway-kids leaped at the pirates. The battle had begun!

When the dust cleared, Patagonia and her boat-pram were halfway up a tree. The pirates were a sorry sight as well. The party food had gone and so had most of their pants. The pirates crept slowly back to their boat.

"What a mess!" cried Jiggling Jim, who had finally escaped from the rigging. "Never mind, I'll teach you how to deal with the highway-kids."

"I can't see how daft disco dancing is going to help," muttered Ziggy.

"I heard that! Do as you're told, you horrid boy!" bellowed Mrs Clatterbottom. "We will not be beaten in battle like that EVER again!"

Chapter 5
Secret Training

"Follow me," ordered Jiggling Jim.

"Follow you where?" demanded Corkella.

Jiggling Jim winked. "To my top-secret training camp," he whispered.

"Follow him, you piffling pirates!" roared Mrs Clatterbottom.

So they did.

When the secret training was over, the pirates felt much braver and very pleased with themselves.

"That was a great kind of dancing," said Ziggy unexpectedly.

Jiggling Jim smiled. "Good. Now, let's get our party food back."

So off they went again. This time, Patagonia Clatterbottom and Jiggling Jim danced down the road singing, "A doo-woppa-diddle, and a bee-boppa-doo, we're gonna make a mess of the highway crew."

Jiggling Jim stopped suddenly and hissed, "Ssssh! Here's the highway-kids' wood."

Chapter 6
Battle Stations!

Patagonia climbed into her boat-pram.
"Oi!" she roared. "You lily-livered load
of land-lubbery highway-hooligans!
Give us back our food.
If you don't we'll …"

"… We'll mash you!" yelled the children.

The trees rustled and out jumped the highway-kids.

"Stand and deliver, whatever the weather! Grrrrrrrrrr!" cried Daisy Mask.

"Pooh! You don't scare me!"
announced the head teacher, and she fired
her cannon.

BOOM! The boat-pram shot
backwards and Patagonia did a nifty
somersault.

She landed upside down, with her legs waving wildly in the air.

"Do that again!" taunted the highway-kids. "It was very funny."

Jiggling Jim winked at the pirates and yelled, "Let battle commence!"

Chapter 7
More Biffing and Baffing

Soon, the ground was littered with groaning highway-kid bodies. Jim's secret training had been a big success. The pirates had flattened the highway-kids with their disco dance moves!

The cowardly-custard highway-kids handed back all the stolen pies and jelly. Then the cheering pirates tied them up in a bundle and stole their pants.

"It's not fair!" cried the highway-kids. "We'll tell Dick Lurkin and he'll get you back!"

Ziggy flashed his joke vampire teeth at Monkey Mask.

"Eek!" squeaked Monkey Mask, and he fainted.

Patagonia Clatterbottom wrote a note.
It said:

Dear Dick Lurkin,

Don't dare bother us
again or we'll give your
highway-kids another
dancing lesson.

Love from
The Dazzling Disco Queen
P. C.

Chapter 8
The Birthday Bash

The party began and everyone was singing 'Happy Birthday' to Mrs Clatterbottom when Dick Lurkin and his highway-kids swarmed onto the deck of the pirate ship.

"We haven't come to fight," said Daisy Mask. "We're very sorry about the pant-stealing."

"We've come to join in the party," said Black Mask, "if you'll let us?"

They played 'Pin the Eyepatch on the Pirate' and 'Musical Cannons', where everyone had to hide in a cannon when the music stopped. Ziggy even fired one, accidentally on purpose, and rocketed Miss Fishgripp far out to sea. Oops!

"This is a great birthday bash," Corkella said to Monkey Mask. "We're glad you all came."

"Us too. You pirates are fun," he told her.

Then the disco started. Patagonia danced with Dick Lurkin, who was a cool mover. He tossed her high into the air. Up, up, up she flew and landed upside down in the crow's nest while Dick Lurkin was still holding her wooden leg! OOPS!

"Oi!" roared Patagonia, swinging down from the crow's nest. "Give me my leg back, you light-fingered shin-stealer. I'm coming to get you!"

Ziggy, Smudge, Flo and Corkella began to laugh.

Mrs Patagonia Clatterbottom was on the war path again!